WEIRD ROOMS

WEIRD ROOMS

PHOTOGRAPHS BY
ALEXANDER VERTIKOFF

TEXT BY
MAL AND SANDRA SHARPE

AN ARCHETYPE PRESS BOOK

POMEGRANATE ARTBOOKS
SAN FRANCISCO

Compilation copyright © 1996 Archetype Press, Inc.

Photographs copyright © 1996 Alexander Vertikoff

Text copyright © 1996 Mal and Sandra Sharpe

Library of Congress Cataloging-in-Publication Data
Sharpe, Mal.
Weird rooms / photographs by Alexander Vertikoff;
text by Mal and Sandra Sharpe.
        p.   cm.
"An Archetype Press Book."
ISBN 0-7649-0010-2
1. Found objects (Art) in interior decoration. 2. Interior decoration—California—History—20th century. I. Sharpe, Sandra. II. Vertikoff, Alexander. III. Title.
NK2115.5.F68S5 1996
747.2'0495–dc20   96-22401
                                            CIP

Pomegranate Catalog No. A855

Published by Pomegranate Artbooks
Box 6099, Rohnert Park, CA 94927-6009

Produced by Archetype Press, Inc., Washington, D.C.
Project Director: Diane Maddex
Designer: Robert L. Wiser
Editorial Assistants: Gretchen Smith Mui and Kristi Flis

Opening photographs: Page 1, "The Museum of Exotica";
Pages 2-3, "The Bird Cage"; Pages 4-5, "Diz's Place";
Pages 6-7, "The Shoe Room"; Pages 8-9, "Milton's House of Toys"; Pages 50-51, "The Grotto"

Printed in Singapore

10 9 8 7 6 5 4 3 2 1

Mal and Sandra Sharpe wish to thank Susan Subtle Din-tenfass, Chris Grampp, Bonnie Grossman, Tracy Johnston, Paul Kilduff, Chris Miller, James Moleski, Rosanna Norton, Sabato, and Joe Wemple.

If you have or know of a weird room, please write to Alexan-der Vertikoff, P.O. Box 2079, Tijeras, NM 87059-2079

CONTENTS

Introduction   6

COLLECTORS

The Smiley Face Room   10

Diz's Place   12

The Kennedy Room   16

The Shoe Room   20

The Fruit Room   22

The Elvis Room   26

Milton's House of Toys   28

The Folk Art Room   32

The Rolls-Royce Room   36

The Museum of Exotica   40

Jayson's Lego City   44

The Monster Room   46

WEIRD ROOMS

The Bird Cage   52

Ken's Spaceship   58

The Room of Burning Souls   60

Karen's World   64

Toru's Cowboy Room   68

The Countess's Room   72

The Formica Room   76

The Valentino Room   80

Bulwinkle's Bedrooms   84

The New Victorian   90

The Grotto   94

This book is about imagination and adventure. It is about people who took their imaginations and turned their ordinary rooms into works of art, even when they did not intend to make art. The adventure was our experience as we tracked down these rooms and then found ourselves sitting in them while their creators, so comfortable in their surroundings, held us spellbound. These rooms grew out of unique points of view held by very different kinds of people.

Many of these rooms did not require piles of money—they just required found objects, paint, and a clever eye. Some rooms were never meant to come into existence, but the clutter just took over. Often these rooms would begin with the haphazard purchase of a solitary object, such as Milton Komisar's spotting a $2.50 rubber Popeye in a junk store window, bringing it home, and ending up twenty-five years later with an entire house crammed with toys. Some of the rooms were willed into existence, for instance, Ken Irwin's spaceship. When he moved into his one-bedroom apartment, he visualized it complete with algae, piranhas, and computer command posts. Some of these rooms grew out of childhood. Bruce Woodbury's smiley face room evokes memories of his happy family. Schultz's space, now filled with teddy bears, is his revenge for the spartan bedroom of his youth.

6

When we started researching this book, we thought that it might be hard to find more than twenty rooms, but they turned out to flow. One person led to another: "Oh, if you think that my room is weird, you should see Simone's." People often asked us what we meant by a "weird room." All we could say was that when you walk in you whisper to yourself, "Wow. This is a weird room." Our colleague, the photographer Alexander Vertikoff, found it puzzling that many of these rooms were not very far from our house in Berkeley, California. Maybe California is just a strange place or maybe if you, dear reader, were to thoroughly investigate your own placid neighborhood, you would find some weird rooms too. We suspect so.

All the colorful folks who opened their doors and shared their rooms with us were inspiring. They have broken through a limited way of seeing. Often, when we would leave their premises and be driving home, we would start babbling about ways to spice up our own house. We hope that they will have the same effect on you.

MAL AND SANDRA SHARPE

COLLECTORS

THE SMILEY FACE ROOM

I remember the day that my dad took my brother, my sister, and me to the store and bought us all smiley faces. I got a smiley face alarm clock. I still have it. It reminds me of my happy family.

A few years ago I set myself a goal of finding a hundred smiley faces, and that was easy. My second goal was two hundred, and that was easy. Then I decided to become known as The Man of a Thousand Faces, and that was hard. Each object had to be different. Obviously this growing collection deserved a room of its own. I was only too happy to oblige. I now own around 1,850 smiley faces.

The origin of the smiley face leads to Mark Rodham, who owned the Button Factory in San Francisco in 1967. A church group would hand out his smiley-face buttons with slogans like "Have a nice day. Get off drugs." San Francisco was getting a lot of attention then, and the face went international. The height of its popularity was 1971—everything in 1971 was smiley. By 1973 it was over. Everyone started to hate those cute little faces. Sometimes I think I collect them because other people detest them. I like to make people groan with my tackiness.

Recently I wanted to know how many smiley faces I had, so I started cataloguing:

Smiley Face Talking Camera. Las Vegas flea market. 1995. $5.

Smile. God Loves You. License plate frame. Clear Lake, Calif. 9/95. $2.

Taco Shop Jesus Calendar. Santa Rosa, Calif. $10.95 (gave guy $10 tip).

I'm Thumbody. Button. Laney flea market, Oakland, Calif. 1993. 25 cents.

I'm about a year behind. Sometimes I think my life would be easier if I didn't have this room.

BRUCE WOODBURY

10

DIZ'S PLACE

The good thing about my bedroom is that it's really dark in here. I have gels covering the windows—red, pink, blue. They come from movie sets I've worked on. I never know what time it is or whether it's rainy or sunny. It's a Hollywood showbiz thing that Norma Desmond would have done, or Norma Dizmond, as I call her.

I have thousands of pictures stapled to the walls. It started with one photo of Robert De Niro; then it spread. One wall is a celebrity wall, and another is a fashion wall. I subscribe to nine magazines, like *Bambino*, *W*, and *Cosmopolitan*, and each month I cut out hundreds of new pictures and staple them to the ceiling. I have more than three thousand pictures of clothes I want to wear some day. I want to be a high-fashion model. I also have a Marilyn shrine, a Wizard of Oz shrine, and a family shrine.

By the way, my father, back in Massachusetts, is a sheriff, and his office walls are covered with photos of famous cops, Mafia guys, and people who have gone to prison. My mother, a hairdresser, has her walls covered with us kids, the Kennedy kids, and the Brady Bunch. We've never had white walls. God forbid!

In my bathroom, or The Can, as I call it, the theme is How to Get Ready. In the kitchen I have two hundred bottles of nail polish in the refrigerator. I don't cook, so I've been able to cover the stove with hundreds of magnets and fill the kitchen drawers with Kewpie dolls and pixies. All my furniture is teeny plastic stuff you can get for ninety-nine cents. The only real thing is a desk. Friends who come to visit from out of town either shake their heads in disbelief or say, "Wow. This is better than Grauman's Chinese Theater."

DIZ McNALLY

12

14

16

THE KENNEDY ROOM

As a poet and an actor, I crave visual stimulation. I was born in Philadelphia, and in my writing I use a lot of Americana. The motif of my living room is early John F. Kennedy. I started this collection when I was seven years old; the first thing I bought was a JFK pamphlet at Knott's Berry Farm. Since then my house has become crammed with thousands of dishes. One's a Norman Rockwell rendition, and another has all the presidents' faces around the edge. Some are so tacky that they don't even look like him. Others have Jack and Jackie in cartoon style with their faces all worn and chipped. I have a revolving, four-sided paperback tree that's stacked with his *Profiles in Courage*.

In a nutshell, the Kennedy image is loaded with great hope and, at the same time, terrible tragedy. He's the comedy and tragedy masks combined. He evokes all things American, all things that inspire promise—until you realize that he's six feet underground in Arlington.

My house is stuffed with objects. I don't know why everybody doesn't overdecorate. How will people know who you are when they walk in your door? I say, "More is more."

I V A N R O T H

THE SHOE ROOM

When I was in the sixth grade my mother would let me buy sample shoes that the big companies would send to our local shoe store. Samples were always size four, so I could wear them. She'd let me buy purple patent-leather shoes and fluorescent shoes.

It was her love of footwear that led to my having this room. Today I own more than five hundred pairs, and even the mayor wants to visit. It's important to surround yourself with things you love. I have a theory: if you can't hang it from the ceiling or nail it to the wall, throw it away.

If you ask a woman about the most significant night of her life, ninety percent of the time she can remember the shoes she was wearing. My favorite antique shoe is one that I found when I was feeding a mule on a deserted fox farm in Petrolia, California. It's black leather with Mexican tooling and a cuff around the toe. People also send me special items such as their wedding shoes.

Back in the early 1970s I worked in a shoe store—that's when shoes had those six-inch platforms. I spent a lot of money flying to trade shows in L.A., where I was befriended by designers such as Joe Famolare; he created those wavy shoes. Joe sponsored my first kinetic sculpture, which was nine feet tall. It was a shoe with eyes that winked, wings that went up and down, and a rotor blade. This led to the big snakeskin shoe you see in my room today. Actually, it's a tricycle. I can sit inside and pedal. It even goes over water. My boyfriend, Ken, and I pedaled the snakeskin shoe 4,012 miles across the country. We're getting ready to pedal the English Channel. I'll be training in this room with one of my other tricycle shoes suspended on a platform.

Some people refer to me as the Imelda Marcos of Humboldt County. It's true. I'd love to get in her closet.

JUNE MOXON

THE FRUIT ROOM

Most people couldn't live this way—a fruit room would be too overwhelming. In fact, I never intended this room to be what it is. It began with a yellow teapot I found in a thrift shop thirty years ago. It was shaped like a pomello, which is a Chinese fruit that looks like a cross between a lemon and a grapefruit. Next, I got a leafy plate with fruit and lobsters, but having just two pieces seemed like nothing. So, I had to collect a whole group.

Then friends started giving me gifts of fruits and vegetables. One day my partner, Eric, and I were walking down Grant Avenue in San Francisco and in a shop we noticed one of those God-awful imitation jade trees with big red fruit. Alone, it was terrible, but when I put it in

the dining room it looked just fine. I love to watch people's expressions. When they walk in, they ask, "Who dusts?" And I say, "Who does?" Many of these fruit pieces come from pre-World War II Japan; some say "Made in Occupied Japan." It's getting tough to squeeze in new items. Pieces that used to go for two dollars now cost forty.

This room can really inspire people. One woman was complaining that she was running out of wall space. I said, "I doubt it." I brought her up to the fruit room, and she replied, "I guess we do have lots of room." When I'm in a house that's very monastic, I say, "It's nice, but your walls are driving me batty." And if I see a shelf with just one fruit or vegetable item, I think, "Yea, God. Don't you have something to go with it?"

BRIAN HOURICAN

23

THE ELVIS ROOM

When I was ten years old, in Waslaco, Texas, I saw *Jail House Rock*. Ever since then, I've been inspired by Elvis. I liked the way he brought people happiness and bought cars for people. He made everyone's dreams come true. Everywhere he went, he was recognized as a good person, not an evil person. All this is reflected in my Elvis room. Nobody comes in here except me—unless they're a special Elvis fan—not even my wife. I seldom sleep in this room, but when I do it seems as if I can hear his music all night.

Each item in this room has a story behind it: the rings, the Elvis watches, the dishes with the sequins. He made a movie called *Roustabout*, about his traveling around the country on a motorcycle; there's a photo of that on the bed. Of course, I have a motorcycle, too. I've tried to base my life on the way he did things. I recently went to an Elvis tribute at the Holiday Inn in Fresno, California. Joan Blackman, who costarred with Elvis in *Blue Hawaii*, was there also. I thought, "Will I ever see her again?" I got the security

guards to take me right up to her. I said, "Joan, you and Elvis inspired me to sing 'The Hawaiian Wedding' at our wedding. Can I take a photo with you?" She was such a warm person. I gave her some hugs and kisses; that photo is in this room. When I went to Memphis, half a million Elvis fans were there, but George Klein, the disc jockey who first put Elvis's music on the air, noticed me in the crowd; it may have been because California people dress more elegantly than people from other states. I have a picture of the two of us on Beale Street.

Every holiday season I play Elvis's Christmas album in front of my house so that everyone can hear it over my lawn. The lawn is shaped like a guitar and is made of hybrid Bermuda grass; the flowers change all year. A couple of times, a long black limo has parked right out front and somebody has rolled down the window to contemplate the yard. I really believe it's Elvis.

VANCE ENRIQUEZ

26

If you get married, you'll probably have kids. If you open a business, you'll probably make money—these are things you do because you have some idea about how the script comes out, but other things that happen in life are totally unexpected.

When I bought a Popeye doll twenty-five years ago, I had no idea that I would end up with rooms stuffed with toys. In 1970 I was looking in a store window in Oakland and saw this old rubber Popeye. I thought, "Boy. That's a nice toy."

I went in and turned it upside down; it read $2.50. I thought, "This is great." I took it home, got a lot of joy out of it, and then bought another toy.

After that, I just don't remember when the grains of sand turned into a beach and this house began to look the way it is today. I became thrilled with buying toys from junk piles. If I saw the same item in its original container, it would bore me. I don't touch anything in stores where everything is laid out, like Kmart. Well, that's not

entirely true—sometimes I'll buy an object at Toys "R" Us. I've paid my dues. Price is important to collectors. If they think that they've overpaid, it'll destroy them. Recently I bought a tin rocket ship for eighty dollars. I was seduced, but then I realized that I hadn't done the right thing. It was a Chinese rip-off of a Japanese design. "What a fool," I told myself. I couldn't live with it, so I sold it for fifteen dollars.

My rooms are all about light and color and shape and process. They don't say, "I'm art," but they're compositions in space. They give me a sense of well-being. Outside the house, on the other side of my fence, I can't control things, but inside I can. If four people visit my living room I cringe, because there's a chance that one of them might move my Charlie Chaplin or my Pinocchio doll, but as soon as they leave, I can run over and put it back. Everything's right again. I don't have a lot of room for other people to sit around in; there's about twelve inches of free space near the TV.

If I were to leave this house or die, I don't picture it becoming a museum, but sometimes I do think about pouring clear acrylic over the entire building so that everything would remain just as it is, forever.

MILTON KOMISAR

29

THE FOLK ART ROOM

We're hunters and gatherers. We like prison art, match-stick art, and tramp art. Once we buy one thing, we have to have three of them, and then it's all over. In this house we feel the spirit and the souls of the people who made these items, even though most of them are anonymous.

These objects are created primarily from the discarded materials of society. You might call it low art, but it's craft, and we think that it documents an era when people had more time on their hands; they could make things because they weren't on their cellular phones. When we buy something like a seven-foot windmill, we have to move everything around, but there's always space for one more piece. Fran's grandmother built this old-style beach house back in the 1940s. We're starting to hang things from the ceiling—they're twenty-five feet high.

In the last five years we've become obsessed with trips. Last year we closed our eyes and pointed at a map of the United States. We ended up going to Missouri for a week. We traveled through all the small towns, hitting the auctions, thrift stores, and flea markets. We bought lots of stuff and shipped it back.

When people come into our living room, it takes their breath away, but we don't know if it makes them go home and throw away their La-Z-Boy chairs. I was brought up by a strict grandmother who was so neat you could bounce a nickel off her bed—maybe this is a rebellion against that lifestyle.

FRAN AND KEITH PUCCINELLI

THE ROLLS-ROYCE ROOM

Just call me Schultz, no first name. Everyone in my German family was named Robert. My mother got sick of it and simplified it to The Schultz. When I turned eighteen, I dropped the "The." While I was growing up on a farm in Nebraska, my stern father didn't allow me to have things like teddy bears; that was "poppycock!" "When you're older, you can have those things." Well, now that I'm older, I have them.

I've lived on a half acre of land here on the Oakland estuary for more than a decade, but the room you're looking at was just finished about a year ago. As a matter of fact, last New Year's Eve this room had only a dirt floor; weeds were growing up all around my 1933 Rolls-Royce Phantom II. The walls, the paintings, the chandeliers, and the ceiling all were here, but there was no floor—just dirt. In fact, on New Year's Eve a friend and I built a big, roaring bonfire, right in the middle of this room.

The room was constructed with salvaged material from old waterfront structures. When they'd tear things down, I'd sneak out in the middle of the night and get the timbers. The trusses in the ceiling came from the Sohio Oil Company. I acquired them when the company finished building portable structures for the Alaska pipeline. The corrugated roof came from the naval supply depot. I told the guy I needed a few pieces. He said, "Schultz, for a fifth of brandy you can have the whole thing." The walls were designed for a walk-in cooler. All the decor is other people's garbage, stuff I found at flea markets. There's a painting here of the famous Japanese woodcarver Ito. He would carve life-like human heads and then use his subjects' real hair for the eyebrows.

So, as you can see, my childhood dreams have come true. I've got the teddy bears, the model airplanes, and the toy cars. But guess what? Having done all this, I've gone into a new psychological mode. Everything you see here—everything I've envied—can now be yours. I'm selling it. I want other people to experience the happiness I had when I found it. The world is a hostile place. I'm keeping this room open for others to share.

S C H U L T Z

THE MUSEUM OF EXOTICA

I used to live in a big mansion in San Francisco's Pacific Heights with twenty-six rooms and a four-story elevator. I bought this place as a storage area; it was an abandoned French laundry. Then I decided that because it was all on one floor and I was getting older, I would move in.

Everything was white. When I started decorating, I went to the auctions and found that the prices on all the old Italian, French, and English furniture had skyrocketed, but nobody seemed to be buying the things from India and Bali, so that's what I got. Belly dancers also turned my taste in this direction. When people heard that I liked peculiar things, they started showing up at my door with weird things to sell. I'd buy an item but tell them that if they wanted it back at the end of a year, they'd only have to reimburse me. (No one's ever come back.)

I'm like the Catholic Church—I acquire. I bought the Laughing Lady who used to greet visitors to San Francisco's historic Fun House. I spend a lot of time walking around this room doing the great reshuffle. I move something here, move something there, put things on top of things; nothing is ever quite finished. I often wake up in the middle of the night with the thought of a new place to put something. My goal is organized clutter.

Oliver Stone wanted to shoot part of his movie on The Doors in here, but there wasn't enough room. There are small sleeping quarters in the back, and I have perpetual house guests. Some friends think that at my age I should be in a nursing home where someone would make my bed and guard my door. But then I wouldn't be talking to all my crazy friends—this is what I like.

JOHN WICKERT

JAYSON'S LEGO CITY

This Lego room began as a small collection on my mother's desk when I was in the second grade. I'm in college now, but I still work on my Lego city. My family moved around a lot, but I could count on the fact that my Lego town would always be there.

I've never used the instruction booklet. Everything is instinctive. I have a space needle, a city hall, a plaza, a cathedral, a mall, a marina, an airport, and tons of apartments. I loved the traffic jams when we'd drive from the country into San Francisco, so there are lots of cars and a double-decker freeway. Whenever I'm in a fast-food restaurant, I take the logos off the cups and use them for signs on enterprises like Taco Bell and Burger King. I made a model of Trump Tower because Trump does the same thing I do. Once a year, as my community grew, I would take all the Lego people out of the buildings and line them up for a census. I kept records of the ratio of men to women and the number of doctors and police officers.

One of my greatest dreams was to work for the Lego Company. In the summer of 1991 I was staying with my great-aunt on Cape Cod. We were planning a trip, and two days before I

turned sixteen I asked her if we could visit Enfield, Connecticut, the American home of Lego. We went and found the factory. A customer representative came down to meet me. I showed him photos of my Lego city, and he was really impressed. When I left the building I was totally filled with joy; I had accomplished an amazing feat before I was sixteen—and on my first trip out of state.

Now that I'm twenty-one, I'm planning to get a master's degree in urban design. To this day, when I go to sleep I have my bed positioned so that it's at the same level as the Lego town. Most people who live where I do see redwood trees through the window, but when I look in that direction, I see the high-rises of my city silhouetted against the moon. It makes me feel safe.

JAYSON ARTHUR McCAULIFF

44

THE MONSTER ROOM

My dad is an art director for movies. A long time ago he made a bunch of monster movies, and they let him keep the monsters. We have a monster room just outside my house, on the other side of the patio. It's my playroom, and my friends think it's neat.

I have severed arms and some big rats. The big ol' wolf is my favorite 'cause he's cool and you can make his legs move with a little cup on the back. My second favorite is the severed head; the mouth is open and he's screaming. On the bottom of his neck is all this gooey stuff. There are some skeletons—some of the bones are real. I also have this big, mutated bear. Once, when my mother was out shopping, four of us dragged him into the house and put him in the front window. When my mom came home, she screamed. She didn't think the mutated bear was funny.

My friends like to sit around the monster room and tell ghost stories. It starts with the biggest kid and then goes around in a circle. The scariest story was "Twenty Drops of Blood." I never come out here in the dark. I always keep the lights on. Someday I'll bet that somebody's gonna turn 'em off.

HUNTER SANDELL

This house used to be owned by Marlene Dietrich's husband, Rudy Sieber, who was an industrial chicken rancher. When Marlene was at home, the maid would move out of the main house and into this guest house. In this room we found lots of dog-food bags stuffed with clippings about Marlene, along with letters she had written to Rudy in German.

KERRY MELLIN
(Mother of Hunter Sandell)

I believe in eerie things, and I'm still afraid of the dark. Early in my career I was working on the set design for a monster movie called *Prophecy*. It was about the environment gone amok with mutated grizzlies in the hills and huge amoebas in the lakes. One day, when the film was over, on my way to the dumpster I noticed this ten-foot mutated bear—they would just throw these things out! I hurried down with a truck and took it home.

That was the beginning of this room. Since then I've collected things, like the head from *Blood Beach Monster*—it has an eyeball that comes out and looks for its prey. My favorite thing is the cheapest, the Pinhead mask from the Ramones' song "Pinhead." It almost looks like Zippy and fits me quite well. I've got some frozen parts—blue cheeks and gums—from the remake of *The Thing*.

I don't want to make this sound like hell; actually, I'm a respectable designer, but we all have our little quirks. My nieces and nephews love to come out here. I always hear lots of rumbling and things moving in the dark. I'm a popular uncle.

B I L L   S A N D E L L
(Father of Hunter Sandell)

49

WEIRD ROOMS

THE BIRD CAGE

One night, before my guest room was painted, I was sleeping here. It was like being inside a white shoe box. I started thinking, "What can I do with this stupid box?" I began visualizing. "It could be a straw hat." Then I thought, "What if I were a canary inside a bird cage?" I liked that idea because it would be easy to paint the walls like a cage. It occurred to me that I could put a cat outside, peering in at my guests. What a trip—my guests confronted by a huge cat! Of course, the guests would feel secure because the cat would be on the other side of the wire. I painted the room, and I shaped the headboard of the bed like a cuttlefish bone. I didn't want the cat's eyes to be too frightening, so I left the pupils out. For the same reason the cat is not drooling.

Visitors often come to my house, peek into my bird cage room, and say, "Oh. I wouldn't want to stay in there." And I say, "It's for guests; they aren't supposed to stay too long."

I grew up near Venice, Italy, which no doubt influenced this room. Venice had an interesting culture: there was no privacy—people lived on top of each other. They had to create privacy, so they used masks, which were worn in carni-

vals. Social intercourse was filled with invention. I love to do murals and trompe l'oeil with subjects from the eighteenth century back to the Greek myths. I like my work to hint at things. Why should a car have four wheels when you can engage viewers and make their brains tick? My joy comes from breaking walls with paint. What you see is not real, but you want to believe it's real. It's a poem.

CARLOS MARCHIONI

53

54

KEN'S SPACESHIP

When I first walked into this apartment, it was just a one-bedroom, 1950s-style place. I had a vision of this space before I moved in. I've had twenty-two other visions that I've built—they've all looked like spaceships.

Everything you see in here I built. The walls and cabinets are made out of duct tape—four thousand rolls of gray duct tape. I used thousands of

pounds of tin foil. I have sixty-one television sets and twenty-three computers in here. Wiring runs all through the ceiling. I don't drive, so I carried everything over here from a store.

One room I call my secondary command center. It has hundreds of plastic gloves filled with water hanging from the ceiling. This creates microsystems of bacteria. You can see the algae growing inside. Each glove is a space colony. I have six robots to protect me from invaders.

My kitchen is a laboratory for the glazes I use on ceramic pottery. I have bottles filled with rotten eggs; the bacteria in the eggs starts to expand, and at a certain point the eggs explode like grenades. They stink like hell. I dry out the eggs and grind them into the powders I use in glazes. The glazes are violet and wine colored.

My bedroom is a loft. Two secret rooms are underneath the bed. One has a full-sized piano. There's a deeper room that only I know about. In my fish bowls I have piranhas; they won't eat goldfish, but they will eat turkey, duck, and beef. You can see the bones. I have flowers on the ceiling; some are real, some are not.

I want the worlds of nature and technology to exist together. If you look out the window from here, all you see are buildings and cars—very few natural areas where I can go to escape. This is my oasis in the brutal, hostile city.

KEN IRWIN

THE ROOM OF BURNING SOULS

This is my shrine room, a nether world, an other-worldly room. At night, the only light in here comes from the objects. I love all the symbolism, but I don't understand why any of it is relevant in the twentieth century.

I have quite a few burning souls in here, animas—figures roasting in hell. Caught in the flames and reaching out, they've always captured my imagination. Religion has been such an inspiration for art. I have Madonnas on one side of the shrine and Christs on the other.

On the wall I have masks, which are the most universal form of folk art; just about every culture has them. But surrealism has gotten into this room, too. The big swordfish is the epitome of kitsch. It represents the whole Tiki culture of southern California in the 1950s. It ties in with bowling and swizzle sticks and Googie-style architecture. The alligator on the ceiling was hanging here long before I installed the shrine.

The big lion is not a religious object; it's the Gilmore lion from the Gilmore Oil Company. It was a Los Angeles icon back in the 1940s and '50s. I don't know where this lion came from. There was the Gilmore Stadium, the Gilmore Drive-in, and all the Gilmore gas stations. The 1950s are so fondly remembered in our culture; all the design ideas seem to recycle well. They may have the strongest influence of any era in this century in America.

BILLY SHIRE

KAREN'S WORLD

I like risk—pushing things to the razor's edge. Look at my living room. It started to evolve when I was sitting in an old Chinese restaurant. The restaurant had those plastic curtains and beads. I decided that I wanted to get that feeling in my house. It took three years.

The connection between colors and shapes interests me. The paintings on my walls come from an organization that encourages mentally handicapped people to create art. These people don't know about cocktail parties and art galleries; they do pure art with no b.s. in between.

When art or objects get fashionable, they don't interest me anymore. Often, when my husband goes away, I stay awake twelve days in a row rearranging the entire house.

I like to have animals around. Animals are basic and direct; they don't play games. For twenty-seven years we lived in these rooms with two ocelots.

Why do I like weird rooms? They're the opposite of fear—you have to learn to live with twists and curves and forget the straight arrow.

KAREN WYSE

TORU'S COWBOY ROOM

About twenty-two years ago I got this idea: I would create a cowboy room where I could watch TV and be a slob. When I was growing up my mother would never let us put our feet on the coffee table, but now I can eat an apple and throw the core across the room, toss peanut shells on the floor, and leave beer bottles where I finish them. This room represents America—the Lone Ranger—but there's another reason for it.

I was born in Japantown. When I was four, I was sent to San Francisco General Hospital with an ear problem. I was there for a month, and because I couldn't speak English, I was very lonely. One day my father came to pick me up with two Caucasian men who, I realized years later, were FBI agents. While I was hospitalized, all the Japanese Americans had been moved into relocation camps. I never returned to my home again. I joined my family in San Bruno, Califor-

nia, where they were living in a stable at a race-track. I'm not glorifying this, but kids can make anything fun. Since then I have always loved the smell of hay, manure, and alfalfa. It brings back memories of playing in the stables.

So when I started this cowboy room, the first thing I did was buy six bales of hay. The night I bought them I slept on them, but they were as hard as bricks and gave me a headache. I've tried to make this room as authentic a bunkhouse as possible, but I'm against guns so I don't have any. A lot of friends come over and want to help me clean up this place, but that would ruin it. This room has gone twenty-two years without being cleaned. Its whole purpose is to let me be a slob. The notion that cowboys have girlfriends can't be true. What woman would live under these circumstances?

TORU SAITO

68

THE COUNTESS'S ROOM

I was born in a castle in Vienna, and my grandfather had a beautiful castle in Hungary, so to me the most important thing in life is to live in lovely surroundings. When I moved into this apartment in Hollywood, I did an intelligent thing: I told the movers, "Bring me only the bed—ten days later, bring the rest." Then I closed my eyes and imagined everything exactly as it is now. I used those ten days to put silks on the wall. I did it all myself with a staple gun.

I got most of my antiques when I lived between Paris and Bangkok. The cousin of the king of Thailand and I were friends as children. When World War II was over, he sent me a ticket and I lived there for seven years. He helped me find all these beautiful things. My Buddha heads are eight hundred years old; in the museums they are set in wood, but I set them in orange stones to remind me of the monks' robes. I decorate them with blue stones to remind me of the sky. I was born a rebel; ever since I was four years old I've wanted to make the world more beautiful. There's a French saying, "Boredom was born one day from uniformity."

One time a gentleman from New York came here to take me out. He looked at his watch and said, "Make it snappy. We have to leave in ten minutes." His nervousness made my hair stand up. I went into the other room and deliberately let him sit in my living room for fifteen minutes. When I came back, he said, "I don't know what's happened. I've never felt so relaxed." I replied, "There are so many things to look at in this apartment that for once in your life you stopped thinking about yourself."

COUNTESS CIS ZOLTOWSKA

THE FORMICA ROOM

When my wife and I bought this house, it had three small rooms and one bath. I built the extra rooms myself, and now it has fourteen. I like the Roman style, so I have a lot of Roman statues and flags. Royal blue, gold, and white are my favorite colors. Before the Roman look I had a Hawaiian atmosphere with a volcano in the front yard and banana trees.

The first chandelier I bought was in Italy; then I got more in Austria. One Christmas my wife, Ann, asked me to go out and buy a Christmas tree, but

I came back with another chandelier. I said, "This is the best Christmas tree I've ever seen."

I got the Marilyn Monroe poster because she attracts a lot of attention. It cost me five hundred dollars to stuff the fish that's over the sofa; behind the fish I had a local artist do something in neon. When I put the canopy over the fish, my wife said, "Who ever saw anything like that?" I said, "It's different. It'll look nice." She got used to it. I have peacock feathers because we used to have a peacock in the back yard. We had a lion, too, but my mother stopped coming over.

One time, at an auction, I was bidding at a distance for a mermaid coffee table, and someone was bidding against me. Finally the auctioneer said, "Wait a minute, Mr. Formica. You're bidding against your own wife." We ended up paying too much, but it proved that she knew my taste. I did this whole house for Ann. She's passed away now, and I miss her.

I have a picture of Hearst's San Simeon castle. He and I had the same idea except that he had more money. In Italian the name Formica means ant. I'm a hard-working person; I take after the ants. If this house caught fire, I'd want to burn with it. I wouldn't feel badly about that at all.

JOE FORMICA

THE VALENTINO ROOM

When I first moved into this house, my husband didn't like it, so I kept doing room after room to make him comfortable. I painted the living room mauve and sea-foam green. "Don't paint anything white," that's my motto.

Some people are totally overwhelmed by my dolls. They walk in and say, "I have to leave now." But none of my dolls looks straight at you; they all glance sideways. They're flirting.

Valentino died the year this house was built. Some people say that they can feel his presence in the tented room I put together. Here's what inspired me: I wrote a book about dolls from 40,000 years ago until today. A Valentino doll was used on the cover—it's one of the most sought-after cloth dolls. I was holding a soirée in my house to promote the book and decided to create a Valentino tent. When I got finished, I added some harem music, and it began to have the atmosphere of Rick's Café in *Casablanca*. To complete the mood, I painted a 360-degree mural of the desert. I used amber-colored lights for ambience.

The space is mesmerizing. It encourages people to fantasize. Often when men walk in, they immediately sink into the pillows and get that look in their eyes—like they're imagining belly dancers. We've held séances in here. Fate is strange. Ten years before I created this room, I started collecting camels—camel inkwells, camel vases, and camel lamps from the 1920s. Now all my camels are in this room. Visitors request this as their guest room; a Javanese prince once slept here. I also have an Asian room inspired by Catherine the Great's son, Peter. It has a luminescent ceiling based on the Dalai Lama's palace.

I got hooked on rooms when I was a child and sat transfixed in front of the TV screen while Jacqueline Kennedy led us on that tour of the White House.

STEPHANIE FARAGO

80

BULWINKLE'S BEDROOMS

This is the bedroom I used to live in when I was married. I often worked seven days a week as a ship welder, so I had little time to repair the cracks in my ceiling. One day I decided to paint something up there. After finishing that, I noticed that the walls were dirty. The paint can was in my hand, so I thought, "Why not?"

Soon the bedroom became a diary of my personal experiences. For instance, if you look closely you'll see a drawing of my respiratory operation. I made all the furniture in this room, including the pantyhose lamp shade. Everything I do is visual diarrhea. I get sick of it, but what can I do?

When I was a kid in Massachusetts, I would never have been allowed to paint anything like this in my bedroom. That's probably why I do it today. My cousin showed up here after twenty-five years and tried very hard not to look around. My relatives were never anxious to bring up the issue of this bedroom.

Just when I was running out of work space in my house, I split up with my wife and ended up in a trailer. I realize now that I never had much use for a house. All I used was the kitchen and the bed; the rest was just storage space. My trailer is on an acre of land in an industrial area of Oakland. I bought it from George, who lived across the street, for eighty dollars. It's just an old 1950s trailer.

I got the idea for painting the inside from a friend who has a basement filled with pinball machines. They're made of wood, they're painted, and they're all lit up. They're called Woodies, and the inside of my trailer reminds me of them—all kinds of shapes and 1950s colors. The painting was also inspired by listening to Lucinda Williams, a country blues singer. She's got that Cajun twang and may not make it into the mainstream, but a lot of the things I wrote on the walls have something to do with her lyrics. Other spaces are just filled up with my thoughts and non-thoughts. Painting the walls like this is a great way to add quality to a poorly built structure.

At night I turn on the Christmas tree lights. Outside, I have my sculpture pieces and my forklift. Inside, even though this trailer isn't very substantial, I feel safe and cozy. It's a great retreat, especially at four in the morning when I can't sleep and I lie here listening to my little radio.

MARK BULWINKLE

88

THE NEW VICTORIAN

My ex-husband and I bought this house as a fixer-upper. You can't beat these Victorian rooms for high ceilings and old moldings. He wanted to restore it to please the next people who'd live here—an investment—but I wanted to live in rooms that would please us. After we split up, I carried on in my own tradition.

Then when Mark Bulwinkle and I got together, I found a strong ally. One rainy day when Mark was feeling restless, I said, "I'll get the paint, if you'll apply it in the hallway." I applied all the background colors, and he had a grand time adding layers of images. This was in the true spirit of Victoriana. Victorian style was heavy with decoration. Wallpaper was pattern piled on pattern. Late at night I would paint the ceilings with clouds, and Mark would add portraits of red dogs and big birds. What we did was harmonious without being slavish to tradition. If you've got a force of nature like Mark around,

why not wallow in it? I did dots, and he did Roy Orbison smoking a cigar.

My mother had always wanted to remodel her kitchen, but she never did. When she died she left some money, and I decided to redo my kitchen. High up I wrote in gold, "Thanks Mom and Dad." I painted the walls yellow, but that looked like a cube of butter, so I scrubbed it with cadmium orange; then I packed the place with Mark's art. It's his work, but I decide where everything goes.

He doesn't live here, but we use this space and the garden as a gallery. I'm a sculptor, and I'm also the curator. These rooms say a lot about the successful collaboration of two very strong-willed people. Visitors often ask, "Wouldn't you like one spot on the wall where you could rest your eyes?" I say, "No. This rests my eyes."

MARCIA DONAHUE

THE GROTTO

I bought my house about twenty-five years ago. After a couple of years I discovered a half-domed cave on the property. It just sat there gathering water. A few years later my wife jokingly suggested that I turn it into a grotto. Although I'm not religious, I started filling it with little figures of the baby Jesus. It still looked bare, so my brother gave me eighty abalone shells. I nailed them around the entrance, and they looked so pretty that friends brought me more and more. Now I've got about nine hundred shells and four hundred religious statues.

It's turned into an ongoing project filled with kitschy Catholic stuff. The grotto gets moist, so plastic flowers work quite nicely; they don't mold or rot. Over the entrance I put up a sign that gives the cave a sense of importance: "In Memory of My Dad, Angelo Carl Ghigliazza. He Was a Good Man."

The grotto may be a little like the catacombs, or, because Italians like me often have matriarchal complexes, it may be a return to the womb. Anyway, when I have the candles lit and I sit here with a glass of grappa, it's a serene escape from reality. When you've taught high school for twenty-five years, you need to get away from it all. Everyone should have a grotto.

ARNE GHIGLIAZZA

94